Circus Throu
The Magic o_ .... Acrobatics

Introduction to Aerial Acrobatics: What is it and how is it different from other circus acts?

When most people think of the circus, they might envision clowns, acrobats, and animals performing amazing feats under a big top tent. But within the world of circus, there is a subculture of performers who specialize in the art of aerial acrobatics. These performers are called aerialists, and their acts involve performing acrobatic maneuvers while suspended in the air by various types of equipment, such as aerial silks, hoops, trapezes, ropes, and more.

Aerial acrobatics is a highly technical and physically demanding art form that requires strength, grace, flexibility, and control. It is a type of performance that combines athleticism with creativity, as aerialists must choreograph their movements to music and create beautiful and captivating visuals for their audience.

What sets aerial acrobatics apart from other circus acts is the use of height and the incorporation of equipment to suspend the performer in the air. The equipment used in aerial acrobatics allows performers to execute complex maneuvers that would not be possible on the ground. For example, aerial silks are long pieces of fabric that can be wrapped around the body, allowing performers to climb, spin, and drop in ways that defy gravity. Aerial hoops, also known as lyra, are metal rings that performers can spin, hang, and contort their bodies through. Trapezes, ropes, and other equipment also allow performers to execute daring and impressive stunts while suspended in the air.

But aerial acrobatics is not just about performing jaw-dropping stunts. It is also about storytelling and creating a connection with the audience. Aerialists use their movements, facial expressions, and music to convey emotions and tell a story through their performance. This creates a unique and intimate experience for the audience, as they are not just watching performers execute tricks, but also witnessing a story unfold before their eyes.

Aerial acrobatics has a long and rich history, dating back to ancient civilizations. In India, performers known as Natya Yogis would perform aerial acts as part of their religious rituals. The ancient Greeks also practiced aerial acrobatics, with performers using ropes and swings to execute daring stunts. In the Middle Ages, performers known as mummers would perform acrobatic acts on wooden beams suspended from the ceiling of a church or castle.

But it wasn't until the modern era that aerial acrobatics became a staple of the circus. In the 19th century, the circus was a popular form of entertainment, and performers began incorporating aerial acts into their shows. This led to the creation of new equipment and techniques, and the evolution of aerial acrobatics as we know it today.

Aerial acrobatics has also influenced other performance arts, such as dance, theater, and even film. Many contemporary dance companies now incorporate aerial techniques into their choreography, and aerialists have performed in productions on Broadway and in movies such as "The Greatest Showman" and "Moulin Rouge!"

In conclusion, aerial acrobatics is a unique and captivating art form that combines athleticism, creativity, and storytelling. It is a type of performance that has a rich history, and has evolved over time to become the awe-inspiring spectacle we know today. Whether you are watching from the ground or suspended in the air, aerial acrobatics is sure to leave you spellbound.

The History of Circus: From Ancient Times to the Modern Era

The circus has been a popular form of entertainment for centuries, with a rich history that spans across continents and cultures. It all began in ancient times, when performers would travel from village to village, entertaining crowds with acrobatic feats, animal shows, and other spectacles.

One of the earliest examples of circus-like performances comes from ancient Rome, where chariot races and gladiator fights were popular forms of entertainment. But it wasn't until the Middle Ages that the first "circus" performances began to emerge. In medieval Europe, traveling performers known as jongleurs would perform acrobatic acts, juggling, and other feats of skill for crowds gathered in town squares and marketplaces.

In the 18th century, the modern circus as we know it today began to take shape. It all started with a man named Philip Astley, a British cavalry officer who had a talent for riding horses. Astley opened a riding school in London, where he would perform tricks and stunts on horseback. He soon began adding other acts, such as acrobats, clowns, and tightrope walkers, and the circus was born.

Astley's circus was an immediate success, and soon other circus troupes began popping up all over Europe. In 1782, Astley opened the first permanent circus building in London, called Astley's Amphitheatre. This was the beginning of the "big top" circus that we know today.

Throughout the 19th century, the circus continued to grow in popularity, with performers traveling across Europe and America to entertain crowds. The introduction of new acts, such as animal shows and aerial acrobatics, helped to make the circus an even more exciting and captivating spectacle.

In the late 1800s, the circus experienced what is known as the "Golden Age of Circus." This was a time when the circus was at the height of its popularity, with enormous circus tents traveling across the country and performers becoming household names. The circus became a symbol of adventure and excitement, and families would gather together to witness the amazing feats of the performers.

But as the 20th century progressed, the circus began to decline in popularity. Changing social attitudes, along with the rise of other forms of entertainment such as television and movies, led to a decline in attendance at circus shows. Animal rights activists also began to protest the use of animals in circus shows, leading many circuses to phase out their animal acts.

Today, the circus continues to exist, although in a much different form than in previous centuries. Many modern circuses have eliminated animal acts and instead focus on aerial acrobatics, clowns, and other human performances. The circus remains a beloved form of entertainment, one that has brought joy and excitement to generations of people.

In conclusion, the history of the circus is a long and fascinating one, dating back to ancient times. From the early days of traveling performers to the modern big top circuses, the circus has captivated audiences and brought joy and excitement to people of all ages. Although the circus has evolved over time, it remains a beloved form of entertainment that continues to amaze and inspire audiences around the world.

Circus in Europe: How the Tradition of Aerial Acrobatics Spread

Circus performances have been a beloved form of entertainment in Europe for centuries. The tradition of circus in Europe dates back to the Middle Ages, where traveling performers would entertain crowds with juggling, acrobatics, and other feats of skill.

It wasn't until the 18th century that the modern circus as we know it began to take shape. In 1768, a British equestrian named Philip Astley opened the first modern circus in London. Astley's circus featured trick riding, acrobatics, and other performances, and it quickly became a sensation.

As the circus became more popular, it began to spread across Europe. Circus companies began touring throughout the continent, performing in cities and towns across the region. By the mid-1800s, the circus had become a staple of European entertainment.

One of the most significant developments in the history of European circus was the introduction of aerial acrobatics. Aerial acrobatics began to gain popularity in the 19th century, with performers using ropes, trapezes, and other equipment to perform daring feats high above the ground. The introduction of aerial acrobatics added a new level of excitement and danger to the circus, and audiences were thrilled by the performances.

One of the most famous circus troupes in Europe during the 19th century was the Circus Renz. The Circus Renz was founded in Germany in 1842 by Ernst Jakob Renz, and it quickly became one of the most popular circuses in Europe. The Circus Renz was known for its elaborate sets, costumes, and performances, and it featured a wide variety of acts, including aerial acrobatics, animal shows, and clowns.

Another famous circus troupe in Europe was the Cirque du Soleil. The Cirque du Soleil was founded in Quebec, Canada in 1984, and it quickly became a sensation. The Cirque du Soleil's shows combined circus acts with theater, music, and dance, creating a unique and captivating experience for audiences.

Today, the tradition of circus in Europe continues, with circuses performing in cities and towns across the continent. The circus has evolved over the years, with many modern circuses focusing on aerial acrobatics, clowning, and other human performances. Some modern circuses have even eliminated animal acts in response to concerns about animal welfare.

In conclusion, the circus has been a beloved form of entertainment in Europe for centuries. The introduction of aerial acrobatics added a new level of excitement and danger to the circus, and performers have continued to push the boundaries of what is possible in the air. Although the circus has evolved over the years, it remains a cherished part of European culture, one that continues to captivate audiences with its thrilling performances and unforgettable spectacles.

The Golden Age of Circus: How Aerial Acrobatics Became a Main Attraction

The Golden Age of Circus is considered to be the period between the late 1800s and early 1900s, when the circus was at the height of its popularity. During this time, the circus became a major form of entertainment in the United States and Europe, with circuses traveling across the country and attracting huge crowds.

One of the most significant developments during the Golden Age of Circus was the rise of aerial acrobatics. Aerial acrobatics had been a part of the circus for centuries, but during the Golden Age, it became a main attraction. Performers began using new equipment, such as the flying trapeze and the aerial hoop, to execute daring stunts high above the ground.

One of the most famous aerialists of the Golden Age of Circus was Lillian Leitzel. Leitzel was a German aerialist who performed with the Ringling Bros. and Barnum & Bailey Circus. She was known for her incredible strength and flexibility, and she would perform a series of stunts on the flying trapeze that left audiences breathless.

Another famous aerialist of the Golden Age was Alfredo Codona. Codona was an American aerialist who performed with the Ringling Bros. and Barnum & Bailey Circus. He was known for his daring and complex maneuvers on the flying trapeze, and he was often referred to as the "king of the trapeze."

Aerial acrobatics became a main attraction during the Golden Age of Circus for a number of reasons. For one, it added a new level of excitement and danger to the circus. Audiences were thrilled by the daring stunts performed high above the ground, and performers became famous for their bravery and skill.

In addition, aerial acrobatics allowed performers to create more elaborate and visually stunning performances. Performers would use music, costumes, and lighting to create a unique and captivating atmosphere for their aerial acts. This added to the overall spectacle of the circus and made it even more popular with audiences.

The Golden Age of Circus began to decline in the mid-1900s, as the popularity of the circus began to wane. But the legacy of the Golden Age lives on, and aerial acrobatics remains a beloved part of the circus tradition. Today, circuses continue to push the boundaries of what is possible in the air, with aerialists performing ever more daring and complex stunts high above the ground.

In conclusion, the Golden Age of Circus was a time of incredible innovation and excitement in the world of circus. Aerial acrobatics became a main attraction during this time, with performers using new equipment and techniques to create thrilling and visually stunning performances. Although the Golden Age may be over, the legacy of the circus lives on, and aerial acrobatics remains a beloved part of this timeless form of entertainment.

Famous Aerial Acrobats: Profiles of the Most Notable Performers in History

Throughout history, there have been many famous aerial acrobats who have captivated audiences with their daring stunts and incredible skill. From the early days of the circus to modern times, aerial acrobats have pushed the boundaries of what is possible in the air, creating unforgettable performances that have left audiences in awe. In this chapter, we will profile some of the most notable aerial acrobats in history.

1. Lillian Leitzel - Lillian Leitzel was a German aerialist who performed with the Ringling Bros. and Barnum & Bailey Circus during the early 1900s. She was known for her incredible strength and flexibility, and she would perform a series of stunts on the flying trapeze that left audiences breathless. Leitzel's most famous stunt was the "One Arm Plange," where she would hold herself up by one arm while doing a full rotation.

2. Alfredo Codona - Alfredo Codona was an American aerialist who performed with the Ringling Bros. and Barnum & Bailey Circus during the early 1900s. He was known for his daring and complex maneuvers on the flying trapeze, and he was often referred to as the "king of the trapeze." Codona's most famous stunt was the "Triple," where he would do three consecutive somersaults in the air.

3. Antoinette Concello - Antoinette Concello was an Italian aerialist who performed during the early 1900s. She was known for her graceful and elegant

performances on the aerial hoop, and she was one of the first female aerialists to achieve international fame. Concello's most famous stunt was the "360," where she would spin around on the aerial hoop while holding herself up with one arm.

4. The Flying Wallendas - The Flying Wallendas are a family of aerialists who have been performing since the early 1900s. They are known for their daring and dangerous stunts on the high wire, and they have performed all over the world. The most famous member of the Flying Wallendas was Karl Wallenda, who performed a tightrope walk between the towers of the Condado Plaza Hotel in Puerto Rico in 1978, just months before his death.

5. Philippe Petit - Philippe Petit is a French aerialist who is best known for his high-wire walk between the Twin Towers of the World Trade Center in 1974. Petit's performance, which was illegal and performed without a safety net, is considered one of the greatest feats of aerial acrobatics in history. Petit has continued to perform high-wire walks around the world, and he is considered one of the most daring aerialists of all time.

6. Nik Wallenda - Nik Wallenda is a member of the Flying Wallendas family, and he has achieved international fame for his high-wire walks across Niagara Falls and the Grand Canyon. Wallenda is known for his calm demeanor and his ability to perform complex stunts while remaining focused and composed.

7. Duo Skyhigh - Duo Skyhigh is a contemporary aerialist duo that has gained fame for their innovative and daring performances on the aerial silks. The duo consists of Anouk Kruithof and Pieter Visser, and they have performed all over the

world, wowing audiences with their breathtaking stunts and intricate choreography.

These are just a few of the many famous aerial acrobats who have left their mark on the world of circus and beyond. Each of these performers brought their own unique style and flair to the art form, and helped to shape the world of aerial acrobatics into what it is today. As we continue to celebrate and appreciate this incredible art form, we can look to these performers as inspirations for what is possible when we push the boundaries of what is possible with the human body.

The Mechanics of Aerial Acrobatics: Understanding the Equipment and Techniques

Aerial acrobatics is a complex and challenging art form that requires strength, flexibility, and skill. To execute the daring stunts and performances that make aerial acrobatics so thrilling, performers rely on specialized equipment and techniques that allow them to fly and spin through the air with ease. In this chapter, we will explore the mechanics of aerial acrobatics, including the equipment and techniques used by performers.

Equipment Used in Aerial Acrobatics

1. Aerial Silks - Aerial silks are long pieces of fabric that are suspended from the ceiling. Performers use the silks to wrap themselves up, spin, and perform acrobatic maneuvers while suspended in the air.
2. Trapeze - A trapeze is a horizontal bar that is suspended from the ceiling. Performers use the trapeze to perform stunts and maneuvers while swinging through the air.
3. Aerial Hoop - An aerial hoop is a circular metal hoop that is suspended from the ceiling. Performers use the hoop to perform stunts and maneuvers while suspended in the air.
4. Static Trapeze - A static trapeze is a horizontal bar that is suspended from the ceiling and does not move. Performers use the static trapeze to perform stunts and maneuvers while suspended in the air.

Techniques Used in Aerial Acrobatics

1. Climbing - Climbing is a fundamental technique used in aerial acrobatics. Performers use their strength and flexibility to climb the silks, trapeze, or hoop, allowing them to reach new heights and perform stunts and maneuvers that would otherwise be impossible.
2. Inversions - Inversions involve flipping upside down while suspended in the air. Inversions require strength and flexibility, and they allow performers to create visually stunning performances that captivate audiences.
3. Drops - Drops are when a performer releases their grip on the equipment and falls through the air before being caught again. Drops require precision and timing, and they add a level of danger and excitement to aerial acrobatics performances.
4. Spins - Spins involve rotating the body while suspended in the air. Spins can be performed on the silks, trapeze, or hoop, and they require balance and coordination.

Safety in Aerial Acrobatics

Aerial acrobatics can be dangerous, and performers must take precautions to ensure their safety. Performers must be trained in proper technique and must use safety equipment, such as crash mats and safety lines, when necessary. In addition, performers must have a strong understanding of their own physical limitations and must know when to stop and rest to prevent injury.

In conclusion, aerial acrobatics is a complex and challenging art form that requires specialized equipment and techniques. From aerial silks to trapeze, performers rely on a variety of equipment to execute their daring stunts and performances. Techniques such as climbing, inversions, drops, and spins are fundamental to aerial acrobatics and require strength, flexibility, and precision to execute. While aerial acrobatics can be dangerous, with proper training and safety equipment, performers can push the boundaries of what is possible in the air, creating unforgettable performances that leave audiences in awe.

Aerial Silk: The Art of Climbing, Wrapping and Dropping on Silk Ribbons

Aerial silks, also known as aerial fabric or aerial tissue, is a popular form of aerial acrobatics that involves performers climbing, wrapping, and dropping on long pieces of fabric that are suspended from the ceiling. Aerial silk performances are visually stunning, combining strength, flexibility, and grace to create beautiful and captivating performances. In this chapter, we will explore the art of aerial silk, including the equipment used, the techniques involved, and the safety precautions performers must take.

Equipment Used in Aerial Silk

Aerial silk performances are typically done using long pieces of fabric that are made of a strong and flexible material, such as silk or nylon. The fabric is suspended from the ceiling using rigging equipment, such as carabiners and pulleys, which allow the performer to climb and spin through the air.

Techniques Used in Aerial Silk

1. Climbing - Climbing is a fundamental technique used in aerial silk performances. Performers use their strength and technique to climb up and down the fabric, allowing them to perform stunts and maneuvers high above the ground.
2. Wrapping - Wrapping involves wrapping the fabric around the performer's body to create a secure hold. Performers use wrapping techniques to create

visually stunning shapes and positions while suspended in the air.

3. Drops - Drops are a more advanced technique in aerial silk, involving releasing the fabric and falling through the air before being caught again. Drops require precision and timing, and they add a level of excitement and danger to aerial silk performances.

4. Spins - Spins involve rotating the body while suspended in the air. Spins can be performed on the fabric, creating visually stunning movements and positions.

Safety in Aerial Silk

Safety is paramount in aerial silk performances, and performers must take a number of precautions to ensure their safety. Performers must be trained in proper technique and must use safety equipment, such as crash mats and safety lines, when necessary. In addition, performers must have a strong understanding of their own physical limitations and must know when to stop and rest to prevent injury.

Performers must also take care to properly rig their equipment, ensuring that it is secure and safe. Rigging equipment should be inspected regularly to ensure that it is in good condition and can support the weight of the performer.

In conclusion, aerial silk is a beautiful and captivating form of aerial acrobatics that requires strength, flexibility, and skill. Performers use long pieces of fabric to climb, wrap, and drop through the air, creating visually stunning performances that leave audiences in awe. While aerial silk can be dangerous, with proper training and safety equipment, performers can push the boundaries of what is possible in the air, creating unforgettable performances that inspire and entertain.

Aerial Hoop: Spinning and Twirling on a Metal Circle

Aerial hoop, also known as lyra or cerceau, is a popular form of aerial acrobatics that involves performers spinning and twirling on a metal hoop that is suspended from the ceiling. Aerial hoop performances are visually stunning, combining strength, flexibility, and grace to create beautiful and captivating performances. In this chapter, we will explore the art of aerial hoop, including the equipment used, the techniques involved, and the safety precautions performers must take.

Equipment Used in Aerial Hoop

Aerial hoop performances are typically done using a metal hoop that is suspended from the ceiling using rigging equipment, such as carabiners and pulleys. The hoop can be made of various materials, such as steel or aluminum, and can come in various sizes and shapes, depending on the performer's preferences and the type of performance.

Techniques Used in Aerial Hoop

1. Climbing - Climbing is a fundamental technique used in aerial hoop performances. Performers use their strength and technique to climb up and down the hoop, allowing them to perform stunts and maneuvers high above the ground.
2. Spinning - Spinning involves rotating the body while suspended in the air on the hoop. Performers can spin in various directions and at various speeds, creating visually stunning movements and positions.

3. Drops - Drops are a more advanced technique in aerial hoop, involving releasing the hoop and falling through the air before being caught again. Drops require precision and timing, and they add a level of excitement and danger to aerial hoop performances.
4. Wraps - Wraps involve wrapping the body around the hoop to create a secure hold. Performers use wrapping techniques to create visually stunning shapes and positions while suspended in the air.

Safety in Aerial Hoop

Safety is paramount in aerial hoop performances, and performers must take a number of precautions to ensure their safety. Performers must be trained in proper technique and must use safety equipment, such as crash mats and safety lines, when necessary. In addition, performers must have a strong understanding of their own physical limitations and must know when to stop and rest to prevent injury.

Performers must also take care to properly rig their equipment, ensuring that it is secure and safe. Rigging equipment should be inspected regularly to ensure that it is in good condition and can support the weight of the performer.

In conclusion, aerial hoop is a beautiful and captivating form of aerial acrobatics that requires strength, flexibility, and skill. Performers use a metal hoop to spin and twirl through the air, creating visually stunning performances that leave audiences in awe. While aerial hoop can be dangerous, with proper training and safety equipment, performers can push the boundaries of what is possible in the air, creating unforgettable performances that inspire and entertain.

Trapeze: From Flying Trapeze to Static Trapeze

Trapeze is one of the oldest and most recognizable forms of circus performance. It involves performers flying and swinging through the air on a horizontal bar, creating beautiful and daring performances that leave audiences in awe. In this chapter, we will explore the history of trapeze, the equipment used, and the techniques involved.

History of Trapeze

The history of trapeze dates back to the mid-19th century, when it was first introduced in circuses and traveling shows in Europe. The first trapeze acts were done using a single bar suspended from the ceiling, and performers would swing back and forth, executing simple acrobatic maneuvers.

As trapeze acts grew in popularity, performers began to experiment with new techniques and equipment, including adding a second bar and incorporating swinging and flying maneuvers. In the early 20th century, the flying trapeze was introduced, which involved performers being launched from one trapeze to another, creating breathtaking performances that pushed the limits of what was possible in the air.

Equipment Used in Trapeze

There are two main types of trapeze: flying trapeze and static trapeze.

Flying Trapeze

Flying trapeze involves performers being launched from one trapeze to another, creating thrilling performances that combine speed, height, and daring acrobatic maneuvers. The equipment used in flying trapeze typically includes safety lines, safety nets, and a series of trapezes that are rigged at different heights.

Static Trapeze

Static trapeze, also known as fixed trapeze or stationary trapeze, involves a performer working on a stationary horizontal bar that is suspended from the ceiling. The equipment used in static trapeze typically includes the trapeze itself, rigging equipment, and safety mats or nets.

Techniques Used in Trapeze

1. Swinging - Swinging is a fundamental technique used in trapeze performances. Performers use their momentum and the swinging motion of the trapeze to perform stunts and maneuvers high above the ground.
2. Releases - Releases involve letting go of the trapeze and falling through the air before being caught again. Releases require precision and timing, and they add a level of excitement and danger to trapeze performances.
3. Catching - Catching involves one performer catching another performer who has been launched from one trapeze to another. Catching requires coordination, timing, and trust between the performers.

4. Static Poses - Static poses involve holding a stationary position on the trapeze, creating visually stunning shapes and positions while suspended in the air.

Safety in Trapeze

Safety is paramount in trapeze performances, and performers must take a number of precautions to ensure their safety. Performers must be trained in proper technique and must use safety equipment, such as crash mats, safety lines, and safety nets, when necessary. In addition, performers must have a strong understanding of their own physical limitations and must know when to stop and rest to prevent injury.

Performers must also take care to properly rig their equipment, ensuring that it is secure and safe. Rigging equipment should be inspected regularly to ensure that it is in good condition and can support the weight of the performer.

In conclusion, trapeze is a thrilling and captivating form of aerial acrobatics that has evolved over the years to include a variety of techniques and equipment. From flying trapeze to static trapeze, performers use strength, skill, and grace to create visually stunning performances that leave audiences in awe. While trapeze can be dangerous, with proper training and safety equipment, performers can push the boundaries of what is possible in the air, creating unforgettable performances that inspire and entertain. Trapeze remains a beloved form of circus performance, and its popularity has led to the creation of new techniques and variations, ensuring that it will continue to evolve and captivate audiences for years to come. Whether you are watching a performer launch through the air on a flying trapeze or gracefully holding a static pose on a stationary trapeze, trapeze performances are sure to leave you breathless and in awe of the strength and skill of these incredible aerial acrobats.

Corde Lisse: The Beauty and Danger of Climbing and Swinging on a Vertical Rope

Corde lisse, also known as aerial rope or Spanish web, is a unique form of aerial acrobatics that involves performers climbing and swinging on a vertical rope that is suspended from the ceiling. Corde lisse performances are visually stunning, combining strength, flexibility, and grace to create beautiful and captivating performances. In this chapter, we will explore the art of corde lisse, including the equipment used, the techniques involved, and the safety precautions performers must take.

Equipment Used in Corde Lisse

Corde lisse performances are typically done using a long rope that is made of a strong and flexible material, such as sisal or manila. The rope is suspended from the ceiling using rigging equipment, such as carabiners and pulleys, which allow the performer to climb and swing through the air.

Techniques Used in Corde Lisse

1. Climbing - Climbing is a fundamental technique used in corde lisse performances. Performers use their strength and technique to climb up and down the rope, allowing them to perform stunts and maneuvers high above the ground.
2. Swinging - Swinging involves the performer swinging back and forth on the rope, using their

momentum to create visually stunning movements and positions.

3. Drops - Drops are a more advanced technique in corde lisse, involving releasing the rope and falling through the air before being caught again. Drops require precision and timing, and they add a level of excitement and danger to corde lisse performances.
4. Wraps - Wraps involve wrapping the body around the rope to create a secure hold. Performers use wrapping techniques to create visually stunning shapes and positions while suspended in the air.

Safety in Corde Lisse

Safety is paramount in corde lisse performances, and performers must take a number of precautions to ensure their safety. Performers must be trained in proper technique and must use safety equipment, such as crash mats and safety lines, when necessary. In addition, performers must have a strong understanding of their own physical limitations and must know when to stop and rest to prevent injury.

Performers must also take care to properly rig their equipment, ensuring that it is secure and safe. Rigging equipment should be inspected regularly to ensure that it is in good condition and can support the weight of the performer.

In conclusion, corde lisse is a unique and captivating form of aerial acrobatics that requires strength, flexibility, and skill. Performers use a vertical rope to climb and swing through the air, creating visually stunning performances that leave audiences in awe. While corde lisse can be dangerous, with proper training and safety equipment, performers can push the boundaries of what is possible in the air, creating unforgettable performances that inspire and entertain. Whether you are watching a performer climb to new heights or gracefully swing through the air, corde lisse performances are sure to leave you breathless and in awe of the strength and skill of these incredible aerial acrobats.

Aerial Straps: The Art of Suspended Strength and Grace

Aerial straps is a form of aerial acrobatics that involves performers using two long straps to create a suspended apparatus. Aerial straps performances are visually stunning, combining strength, flexibility, and grace to create beautiful and captivating performances. In this chapter, we will explore the art of aerial straps, including the equipment used, the techniques involved, and the safety precautions performers must take.

Equipment Used in Aerial Straps

Aerial straps performances are typically done using two long straps made of a strong and flexible material, such as nylon or silk. The straps are suspended from the ceiling using rigging equipment, such as carabiners and pulleys, which allow the performer to create a suspended apparatus.

Techniques Used in Aerial Straps

1. Suspended Positions - Suspended positions involve the performer holding static poses while suspended in the air by the straps. These positions require strength, flexibility, and grace to create visually stunning shapes and movements.
2. Drops - Drops are a more advanced technique in aerial straps, involving releasing one or both of the straps and falling through the air before being caught again. Drops require precision and timing, and they add a level of excitement and danger to aerial straps performances.

3. Rolls - Rolls involve the performer rolling and twisting the body while suspended in the air by the straps. These movements require strength, flexibility, and coordination to execute properly.

Safety in Aerial Straps

Safety is paramount in aerial straps performances, and performers must take a number of precautions to ensure their safety. Performers must be trained in proper technique and must use safety equipment, such as crash mats and safety lines, when necessary. In addition, performers must have a strong understanding of their own physical limitations and must know when to stop and rest to prevent injury.

Performers must also take care to properly rig their equipment, ensuring that it is secure and safe. Rigging equipment should be inspected regularly to ensure that it is in good condition and can support the weight of the performer.

In conclusion, aerial straps is a beautiful and captivating form of aerial acrobatics that requires strength, flexibility, and skill. Performers use two long straps to create a suspended apparatus, allowing them to hold static positions, execute drops, and perform rolls while suspended in the air. While aerial straps can be dangerous, with proper training and safety equipment, performers can push the boundaries of what is possible in the air, creating unforgettable performances that inspire and entertain. Whether you are watching a performer hold a suspended pose or gracefully execute a roll, aerial straps performances are sure to leave you breathless and in awe of the strength and skill of these incredible aerial acrobats.

Aerial Net: A Unique and Challenging Form of Aerial Acrobatics

Aerial net is a unique and challenging form of aerial acrobatics that involves performers using a suspended net to create a suspended apparatus. Aerial net performances are visually stunning, combining strength, flexibility, and grace to create beautiful and captivating performances. In this chapter, we will explore the art of aerial net, including the equipment used, the techniques involved, and the safety precautions performers must take.

Equipment Used in Aerial Net

Aerial net performances are typically done using a large, suspended net made of a strong and flexible material, such as nylon or polypropylene. The net is suspended from the ceiling using rigging equipment, such as carabiners and pulleys, which allow the performer to create a suspended apparatus.

Techniques Used in Aerial Net

1. Climbing - Climbing is a fundamental technique used in aerial net performances. Performers use their strength and technique to climb up and down the net, allowing them to perform stunts and maneuvers high above the ground.
2. Swinging - Swinging involves the performer swinging back and forth on the net, using their momentum to create visually stunning movements and positions.
3. Drops - Drops are a more advanced technique in aerial net, involving releasing the net and falling

through the air before being caught again. Drops require precision and timing, and they add a level of excitement and danger to aerial net performances.

4. Static Poses - Static poses involve holding a stationary position on the net, creating visually stunning shapes and positions while suspended in the air.

Safety in Aerial Net

Safety is paramount in aerial net performances, and performers must take a number of precautions to ensure their safety. Performers must be trained in proper technique and must use safety equipment, such as crash mats and safety lines, when necessary. In addition, performers must have a strong understanding of their own physical limitations and must know when to stop and rest to prevent injury.

Performers must also take care to properly rig their equipment, ensuring that it is secure and safe. Rigging equipment should be inspected regularly to ensure that it is in good condition and can support the weight of the performer.

In conclusion, aerial net is a unique and challenging form of aerial acrobatics that requires strength, flexibility, and skill. Performers use a suspended net to climb and swing through the air, creating visually stunning performances that leave audiences in awe. While aerial net can be dangerous, with proper training and safety equipment, performers can push the boundaries of what is possible in the air, creating unforgettable performances that inspire and entertain. Whether you are watching a performer climb to new heights or gracefully swing through the air on a suspended net, aerial net performances are sure to leave you breathless and in awe of the strength and skill of these incredible aerial acrobats.

Aerial Cube: Performing Acrobatics on a 3-Dimensional Cube Structure

Aerial cube is a form of aerial acrobatics that involves performers using a suspended 3-dimensional cube structure to create a suspended apparatus. Aerial cube performances are visually stunning, combining strength, flexibility, and grace to create beautiful and captivating performances. In this chapter, we will explore the art of aerial cube, including the equipment used, the techniques involved, and the safety precautions performers must take.

Equipment Used in Aerial Cube

Aerial cube performances are typically done using a suspended cube structure made of a strong and lightweight material, such as aluminum or steel. The cube is suspended from the ceiling using rigging equipment, such as carabiners and pulleys, which allow the performer to create a suspended apparatus.

Techniques Used in Aerial Cube

1. Climbing - Climbing is a fundamental technique used in aerial cube performances. Performers use their strength and technique to climb up and down the cube structure, allowing them to perform stunts and maneuvers high above the ground.
2. Static Poses - Static poses involve holding a stationary position on the cube structure, creating visually stunning shapes and positions while suspended in the air.

3. Rolling - Rolling involves the performer rolling and twisting the body while suspended on the cube structure. These movements require strength, flexibility, and coordination to execute properly.
4. Drops - Drops are a more advanced technique in aerial cube, involving releasing the cube structure and falling through the air before being caught again. Drops require precision and timing, and they add a level of excitement and danger to aerial cube performances.

Safety in Aerial Cube

Safety is paramount in aerial cube performances, and performers must take a number of precautions to ensure their safety. Performers must be trained in proper technique and must use safety equipment, such as crash mats and safety lines, when necessary. In addition, performers must have a strong understanding of their own physical limitations and must know when to stop and rest to prevent injury.

Performers must also take care to properly rig their equipment, ensuring that it is secure and safe. Rigging equipment should be inspected regularly to ensure that it is in good condition and can support the weight of the performer.

In conclusion, aerial cube is a unique and challenging form of aerial acrobatics that requires strength, flexibility, and skill. Performers use a suspended 3-dimensional cube structure to climb and perform stunts and maneuvers high above the ground. While aerial cube can be dangerous, with proper training and safety equipment, performers can push the boundaries of what is possible in the air, creating unforgettable performances that inspire and entertain. Whether you are watching a performer hold a suspended pose on the cube structure or gracefully execute a roll, aerial cube performances are sure to leave you breathless and in awe of the strength and skill of these incredible aerial acrobats.

The Evolution of Aerial Acrobatics: From Traditional to Contemporary Acts

Aerial acrobatics has come a long way since its inception. Over the years, it has evolved and transformed into a dynamic and innovative art form. In this chapter, we will explore the evolution of aerial acrobatics from traditional to contemporary acts.

Traditional Aerial Acrobatics

Traditional aerial acrobatics has its roots in the circus and variety shows of the past. Performers would use simple equipment such as ropes, ladders, and trapezes to create suspended apparatuses for their performances. Acts were focused on strength, agility, and grace, and included classic techniques such as climbs, drops, and swings.

As aerial acrobatics gained popularity, new equipment was developed to enhance performances. The addition of safety lines, crash mats, and better rigging equipment made performances safer and allowed performers to push the limits of what was possible in the air.

Contemporary Aerial Acrobatics

Today, aerial acrobatics has evolved into a dynamic and innovative art form that encompasses a wide variety of techniques and styles. Contemporary aerial acrobatics combines elements of dance, theater, and acrobatics to create visually stunning and emotionally powerful performances.

New equipment such as aerial silks, aerial hoops, aerial cubes, and aerial nets have allowed performers to create new and exciting aerial apparatuses. Performers now incorporate music, lighting, and costumes to enhance their performances and create a complete visual experience for the audience.

Contemporary aerial acrobatics has also embraced new techniques and styles that push the boundaries of what is possible in the air. Performers now use a combination of strength, flexibility, and creativity to create performances that are as beautiful as they are daring.

In conclusion, aerial acrobatics has come a long way from its traditional roots in the circus and variety shows of the past. Today, it is a dynamic and innovative art form that combines strength, agility, grace, and creativity to create visually stunning performances. As equipment and techniques continue to evolve, it is clear that aerial acrobatics will continue to push the boundaries of what is possible in the air, inspiring and entertaining audiences around the world.

How Aerial Acrobatics Has Influenced Other Performance Arts

Aerial acrobatics has become a highly respected and popular performance art that has influenced other performance arts in a variety of ways. In this chapter, we will explore the impact of aerial acrobatics on other performance arts and how it has helped to shape and transform the world of entertainment.

Dance

Aerial acrobatics has had a significant impact on the world of dance, with performers incorporating aerial techniques and apparatuses into their performances. Aerial silks, for example, have become a popular addition to modern dance performances, allowing dancers to create visually stunning and dynamic movements while suspended in the air. Aerial acrobatics has also inspired new forms of dance, such as aerial dance, which combines elements of aerial acrobatics with contemporary dance styles.

Circus

Aerial acrobatics has always been an integral part of the circus, and it has continued to influence and shape the world of circus performances. The use of new apparatuses and techniques has allowed performers to create new and exciting acts, pushing the boundaries of what is possible in the air. Aerial acrobatics has also inspired the creation of new circus styles, such as contemporary circus, which combines elements of dance, theater, and acrobatics to create visually stunning and emotionally powerful performances.

Theater

Aerial acrobatics has had a significant impact on the world of theater, with performers incorporating aerial techniques into their performances to create visually stunning and dynamic shows. Aerial hoops, for example, have become a popular addition to theatrical performances, allowing performers to create beautiful and graceful movements while suspended in the air. Aerial acrobatics has also inspired the creation of new theatrical styles, such as aerial theater, which combines elements of aerial acrobatics, dance, and theater to create immersive and engaging performances.

Film and Television

Aerial acrobatics has even made its way into the world of film and television, with performers creating dynamic and visually stunning performances on camera. Aerial acrobatics has been featured in a variety of films and television shows, from action movies to music videos, showcasing the beauty and grace of this incredible art form to audiences around the world.

In conclusion, aerial acrobatics has had a significant impact on other performance arts, inspiring new techniques, apparatuses, and styles. From dance to circus, theater to film and television, aerial acrobatics has transformed the world of entertainment, inspiring performers and audiences alike with its beauty, grace, and daring. As aerial acrobatics continues to evolve and innovate, it is clear that it will continue to inspire and influence the world of entertainment, shaping and transforming it for years to come.

Training for Aerial Acrobatics: What it Takes to Become an Aerialist

Aerial acrobatics is a highly demanding and physically challenging art form that requires years of training and practice to master. In this chapter, we will explore in detail the training required to become an aerialist, including the physical and mental skills needed to perform at a high level.

Physical Conditioning

Aerial acrobats must have exceptional physical strength, flexibility, and endurance to perform their routines. Training for aerial acrobatics typically involves a combination of strength training, cardio, and flexibility exercises. Strength training focuses on building core and upper body strength to support the weight of the performer while in the air. Cardiovascular exercise is important for building endurance, while flexibility training helps performers achieve the necessary range of motion for aerial maneuvers.

Strength training includes exercises such as pull-ups, chin-ups, push-ups, and planks. These exercises work on building upper body strength, as well as core strength, which is essential for maintaining balance and control while in the air. Cardiovascular exercise includes activities such as running, cycling, and swimming, which are important for building endurance.

Flexibility training includes exercises such as stretching and yoga, which help to improve range of motion and prevent injury. Aerial acrobats must have a high level of flexibility to perform their routines, and often engage in targeted stretching routines to improve their range of motion.

Mental Preparation

In addition to physical conditioning, aerialists must also be mentally prepared to perform. Aerial acrobatics requires intense focus and concentration, and performers must be able to maintain their composure even when performing high above the ground. Mental preparation also involves developing trust and communication with other members of the performance team, including riggers and spotters.

To develop mental strength and focus, aerialists often engage in activities such as meditation and visualization. These practices help performers stay centered and focused, even in high-pressure situations.

Technique Training

Training for aerial acrobatics also involves learning the techniques and maneuvers necessary for performances. This includes proper climbing and descending techniques, as well as more advanced maneuvers such as drops and rolls. Learning proper technique is essential for both safety and performance quality.

Technique training often involves working with an experienced aerial coach, who can provide guidance and feedback on proper technique. Aerialists often start by learning basic climbs and descents, and gradually progress to more advanced maneuvers as their skills improve.

Rigging and Safety Training

Aerial acrobats must also be trained in rigging and safety procedures to ensure their own safety and the safety of others. Performers must understand how to properly rig their equipment, including how to tie knots and use rigging hardware. Safety training includes understanding how to properly use safety lines and crash mats, as well as how to communicate with riggers and spotters during performances.

To ensure safety, aerialists must also be trained to identify potential hazards and mitigate risks. This includes understanding the limits of their equipment, as well as the physical limits of their own bodies.

In conclusion, becoming an aerialist requires years of dedicated training and practice, both physically and mentally. Performers must develop exceptional physical strength, endurance, and flexibility, as well as mental focus and concentration. Learning proper technique and safety procedures is also essential for both safety and performance quality. Rigorous training and preparation are necessary to achieve success in the highly demanding and physically challenging world of aerial acrobatics.

The Dangers of Aerial Acrobatics: How Safety Measures Have Changed Over Time

Aerial acrobatics is a breathtaking and awe-inspiring art form, but it is also one of the most dangerous. The physical demands of the art, combined with the height at which performers work, make it essential to prioritize safety. In this chapter, we will explore the history of safety measures in aerial acrobatics and how they have evolved over time.

Early Safety Measures

In the early days of aerial acrobatics, safety measures were minimal or non-existent. Performers often worked without safety lines or crash mats, and injuries were common. However, as the popularity of aerial acrobatics grew, so too did the need for improved safety measures.

One of the first significant safety innovations was the invention of the safety net, which allowed performers to practice their routines with greater confidence. However, safety nets were not always reliable, and performers continued to suffer serious injuries.

Improvements in Safety

As the art of aerial acrobatics continued to develop, so too did safety measures. In the mid-20th century, the use of safety lines became standard practice, allowing performers to work at greater heights with reduced risk. Additionally, advancements in rigging technology allowed for more secure and reliable rigging of aerial equipment.

Today, safety measures in aerial acrobatics are highly advanced, with strict regulations and guidelines in place to ensure the safety of performers and audience members alike. Performers are required to undergo rigorous training and certification processes, and equipment must be regularly inspected and maintained.

Some of the safety measures used in aerial acrobatics today include:

- Safety lines: Performers are often attached to safety lines or harnesses that prevent them from falling to the ground in the event of a mistake or equipment failure.
- Crash mats: Thick, cushioned mats are used to cushion falls and reduce the risk of injury.
- Spotting: Other members of the performance team, such as riggers and spotters, work to ensure the safety of the performer and prevent accidents from occurring.
- Equipment checks: All equipment, including rigging hardware, ropes, and fabrics, must be regularly inspected and maintained to ensure its safety and reliability.

While aerial acrobatics is a thrilling and beautiful art form, it is not without risk. However, as the art has evolved, so too have safety measures, leading to a much safer and more secure practice. Today's aerial acrobats work in an environment that is designed to keep them safe, allowing them to push the limits of their art while minimizing the risk of injury. As the art continues to develop and evolve, we can expect to see even further improvements in safety measures, ensuring that performers and audience members can continue to enjoy the beauty and excitement of aerial acrobatics for generations to come.

Aerial Acrobatics Around the World: Unique Styles and Traditions

Aerial acrobatics is a truly global art form, with unique styles and traditions found in countries all over the world. In this chapter, we will explore some of the most distinctive aerial acrobatics styles and traditions from around the world, giving you a glimpse into the diverse and fascinating world of aerial acrobatics.

China: Chinese Pole Acrobatics

Chinese pole acrobatics is a traditional Chinese art form that involves performing acrobatic maneuvers on a tall, vertical pole. Performers use their upper body strength to climb up and down the pole, as well as perform flips and other acrobatic maneuvers. The poles are often decorated with colorful ribbons, adding to the visual spectacle of the performance. Chinese pole acrobatics has a long history in China, dating back to the Tang dynasty over 1,000 years ago. Today, it is often performed as part of traditional Chinese festivals and celebrations.

Russia: Aerial Straps

Aerial straps is a Russian aerial acrobatics style that involves performing acrobatic maneuvers on two suspended straps. Performers use their upper body strength to perform a variety of flips and twists, often incorporating dance and choreography into their routines. Aerial straps has a strong presence in Russia and is often performed as part of circus shows and competitions. It is known for its strength and grace, requiring performers to have exceptional upper body strength and control.

Mexico: Aerial Rope

Aerial rope, also known as corde lisse, is a Mexican aerial acrobatics style that involves performing acrobatic maneuvers on a long, vertical rope. Performers use their upper body strength to climb the rope and perform a variety of twists and flips while suspended in the air. Aerial rope has a long history in Mexico and is often performed as part of traditional festivals and celebrations. It is known for its fluidity and grace, requiring performers to have excellent technique and control.

France: Aerial Hoop

Aerial hoop, also known as lyra, is a French aerial acrobatics style that involves performing acrobatic maneuvers on a suspended metal hoop. Performers use their upper body strength to perform a variety of flips, twists, and turns, often incorporating dance and choreography into their routines. Aerial hoop has a strong presence in the French circus tradition and is often performed as part of contemporary circus shows. It is known for its beauty and elegance, requiring performers to have excellent flexibility and strength.

India: Mallakhamb

Mallakhamb is an Indian aerial acrobatics style that involves performing acrobatic maneuvers on a thick wooden pole. Performers use their upper body strength to climb the pole and perform a variety of twists and flips while suspended in the air. The art form has been practiced in India for centuries, and is often performed in festivals and competitions. Mallakhamb is known for its strength and agility, requiring performers to have exceptional upper body strength and coordination.

Aerial acrobatics is a diverse and fascinating art form, with unique styles and traditions found all over the world. Each country and culture brings its own unique perspective and techniques to aerial acrobatics, resulting in a rich tapestry of styles and approaches. Whether it's the Chinese pole acrobatics of China, the aerial straps of Russia, or the aerial hoop of France, each style of aerial acrobatics offers its own unique challenges and rewards. By exploring the aerial acrobatics traditions of different countries, we gain a deeper appreciation for the art form as a whole and the incredible athleticism and creativity of its practitioners.

The Future of Aerial Acrobatics: Innovations and Advancements in Technology

As aerial acrobatics continues to evolve and grow in popularity, advancements in technology are playing a crucial role in shaping its future. In this chapter, we will explore some of the most exciting innovations and advancements in technology that are transforming the world of aerial acrobatics.

Virtual Reality and Augmented Reality

Virtual reality (VR) and augmented reality (AR) technologies have the potential to revolutionize the way we experience and train for aerial acrobatics. With VR, performers can experience and practice complex maneuvers in a safe and controlled virtual environment before attempting them in the real world. AR can enhance the performer's experience by overlaying digital information onto the physical world, allowing performers to visualize and plan their routines more effectively.

Wireless Sensor Technology

Wireless sensor technology is being used to create wearable devices that can track and monitor a performer's movements in real-time. This technology can be used to analyze and improve technique, as well as prevent injuries by alerting performers to potential risks or overuse injuries.

Advanced Rigging Systems

Advancements in rigging systems are allowing performers to push the boundaries of what is possible in aerial acrobatics. Complex rigging systems that allow performers to move in three-dimensional space, as well as computer-controlled systems that can create complex choreography, are becoming more common in the world of aerial acrobatics.

Innovative Equipment

Advancements in material science and engineering are creating new and innovative equipment for aerial acrobatics. From lighter and stronger rigging hardware to new materials for aerial silks and hoops, these advancements are allowing performers to create more daring and impressive routines.

New Forms of Collaboration

As aerial acrobatics becomes more popular, performers are finding new and innovative ways to collaborate and push the boundaries of the art form. Collaborations between aerial acrobatics performers and other artists, such as dancers and musicians, are becoming more common, resulting in breathtaking performances that blend different art forms together in new and exciting ways.

As we look to the future of aerial acrobatics, it's clear that advancements in technology will continue to play a crucial role in shaping the art form. Whether it's through virtual reality and augmented reality, wireless sensor technology, advanced rigging systems, innovative equipment, or new forms of collaboration, these advancements are allowing performers to push the boundaries of what is possible in aerial acrobatics. As the world of aerial acrobatics continues to evolve, we can expect to see even more exciting and innovative developments in the years to come.

Conclusion: The Art and Magic of Aerial Acrobatics

Aerial acrobatics is a captivating and awe-inspiring art form that has captured the hearts of audiences for centuries. From the daring and death-defying feats of early aerialists to the intricate and graceful performances of modern aerialists, the world of aerial acrobatics has continually evolved and grown in popularity.

Throughout this book, we have explored the rich history of aerial acrobatics, its evolution across different cultures and countries, and the various forms and techniques that make it such a unique and fascinating art form. We have also delved into the training and safety measures necessary to become an aerialist, as well as the challenges and dangers that come with this incredible art form.

What makes aerial acrobatics so magical is the way it combines strength, grace, and daring in a way that is both beautiful and captivating. It's a true test of physical and mental strength, requiring performers to not only have incredible strength and endurance, but also the skill and technique to execute complex maneuvers with precision and grace.

At its core, aerial acrobatics is a celebration of the human spirit, pushing the boundaries of what is possible and inspiring us to dream big and reach for the impossible. It's a testament to the power of creativity and imagination, and the transformative effect that art can have on our lives.

As we look to the future of aerial acrobatics, we can expect to see even more exciting developments and advancements in technology that will continue to push the art form to new heights. But no matter how much technology advances, the true magic of aerial acrobatics will always lie in the performers themselves, and the incredible strength, skill, and artistry they bring to the stage.

So whether you're a seasoned aerialist or simply a curious observer, we hope this book has inspired you to appreciate the beauty and magic of aerial acrobatics, and to continue to support this incredible art form for generations to come.

Thank you for taking the time to read this book on aerial acrobatics. We hope that you found it informative, engaging, and entertaining.

If you enjoyed the book, we would greatly appreciate it if you could take a few moments to leave a positive review. Your feedback helps us to improve and continue creating content that you find valuable.

Thank you again for your support, and we hope that this book has inspired you to appreciate the beauty and magic of aerial acrobatics.

Freya and Viktor

About the author:

Freya Adeline Mercer is a gifted writer and adventurer, born to a Scottish father and an Icelandic mother. Her unique upbringing provided her with an appreciation for cultural diversity and a passion for storytelling, which she honed throughout her childhood.

After completing her education in England, where she earned degrees in History and Literature, Freya decided to embark on an adventure, traveling to the United States. It was there that she met her fiancé, a talented circus artist from Ukraine, and they fell in love.

Freya and her fiancé Viktor, along with their two children, now travel the world with the circus, immersing themselves in different cultures and experiences. To support their lifestyle, Freya works as a virtual assistant and author, which allows her to work remotely and continue pursuing her passion for writing.

In her free time, Freya enjoys practicing circus arts and reading. Her love for literature is evident in her writing, which has been praised for its captivating storytelling and unique perspectives. Her travel experiences also influence her writing, as she often draws inspiration from the places she visits and the people she meets.

Despite the challenges of living a nomadic lifestyle, Freya is grateful for the experiences and opportunities that her travels have provided her. She hopes to continue to explore new cultures and write stories that inspire and engage readers for years to come.

Printed in Great Britain
by Amazon